LIBRARY
ANDERSON ELEMENTARY SCHOOL

Presented to

ANDY ANDERSON SCHOOL LIBRARY

by

MARK WALCOFF

Miss Buzzini's Third Grade

BOOK FAIR 1967-1968

With Washington
at Valley Forge

Throughout the long, cruel winter of 1777, hundreds of your fellow soldiers are dying of cold, disease, and starvation. Camping on the ice-covered ground of eastern Pennsylvania, Washington's army is keeping watch over the British in Philadelphia. Somehow, you survive the terrible winter. With the arrival of spring there comes help from the French and hope of victory for the rebel Americans.

Building America

LIBRARY
ANDERSON ELEMENTARY SCHOOL

With Washington at Valley Forge

by Judith M. Spiegelman

Illustrated by Albert Micale

G. P. Putnam's Sons   New York

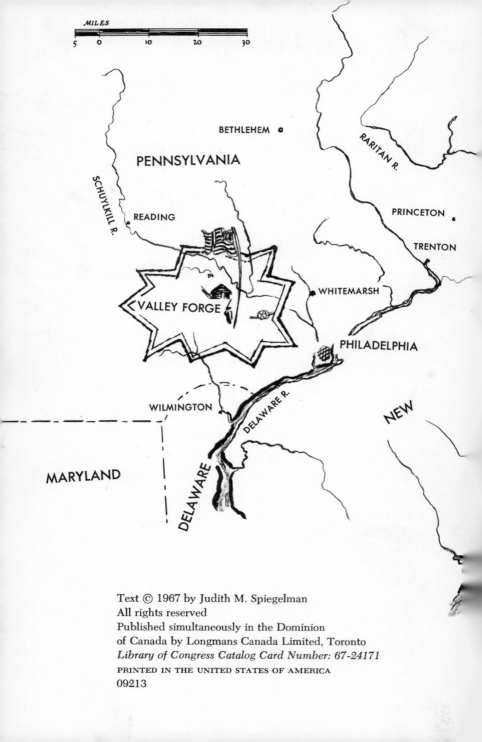

Text © 1967 by Judith M. Spiegelman
All rights reserved
Published simultaneously in the Dominion
of Canada by Longmans Canada Limited, Toronto
Library of Congress Catalog Card Number: 67-24171
PRINTED IN THE UNITED STATES OF AMERICA
09213

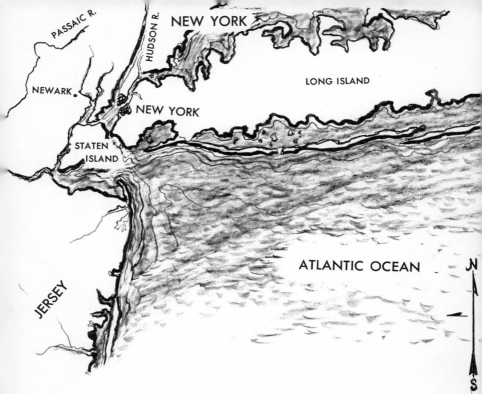

It is December, 1777, and bitter cold. You are a farm boy of fifteen marching with General Washington's army along the frozen roads of Pennsylvania. An icy wind cuts through your thin, homespun jacket. You have been wearing this same jacket ever since you left your grandfather's Connecticut farm two years ago. Far ahead you can see General Washington, your leader in the fight to free your new nation, the United States of America, from British rule.

5

You can feel the sharp ridges of the frozen road through the thin soles of your shoes tied to your feet with cord. Most of the other nine thousand soldiers have only rags or strips of blanket wrapped around their feet. With every step they take, the ice cuts into their feet. You can see bloody footprints in the snow.

You hear the clatter of horses' hoofs on the ice as a gray-cloaked man with fearless blue

eyes rides up. It is General Washington, coming to ask the colonel commanding your regiment, "How is it, sir, I have tracked the march of your troops by these bloodstains? Weren't there shoes enough in the commissary store?"

"Sir," comes the answer, "supplies were exhausted before my regiment's turn was reached."

You hear the General mutter, "Poor devils." His jaw is set in a hard line as he slowly moves his gray stallion on. He has begged the governors of the thirteen colonies to send their men shoes, clothing and food. So far no supplies have come.

Painfully, the half-frozen army moves on until you can see the gray waters of the Schuylkill River. Valley Forge, your camp for the winter, lies on the other side. At the crossroads, Washington orders a scout to climb up the tallest chestnut tree. From its top, the scout sees that no Redcoats are coming. Safe from attack for the moment, Washington orders your army to cross the river.

The first regiments sink wagons end to end
in the shallow water. Then your regiment
places boards and planks across the wagon
tops. Over this wagon-top bridge, the entire
army crosses single file.

9

At four o'clock, drums signal your regiment on the last three miles to Valley Forge. The Tarheels, boys from North Carolina, lead the way. Behind them you can see young Lafayette, the French noble, his red hair powdered white with falling snow. He is urging his exhausted men up the last few yards to the top of the hill. Your buddy slips and stumbles, cutting himself on the ice. Somehow you help pull him the last few steps to the top of the hill.

Here lies Valley Forge. It is a rolling plain covered with snow. You can see the charred remains of houses burned by the British. Oaks and hemlocks crusted with ice stand guard. There is nothing else in sight.

If only you could just lie down in the snow and sleep! But no one can rest just yet. First you must help build huts for the sick and wounded. Otherwise they would surely die in this cold. You are chosen to chop down some small fir trees, while others notch logs and spread hemlock branches for a roof. At last the wounded are sheltered.

In the swirling snows, you join men who are gathering twigs and branches for campfires. Some fires are already burning, but the wood is green and gives off big clouds of gray smoke.

Men huddle around the fires, coughing, rubbing their smarting eyes.

Your regiment is lucky, for the people of Connecticut have supplied you boys with tents. Twice you and the other Connecticut soldiers try to pitch your tent, and twice the strong wind pushes it down. The third time you pitch it firmly in the snow. Now you can see that it won't give much shelter, for the tent flaps are worn and tattered.

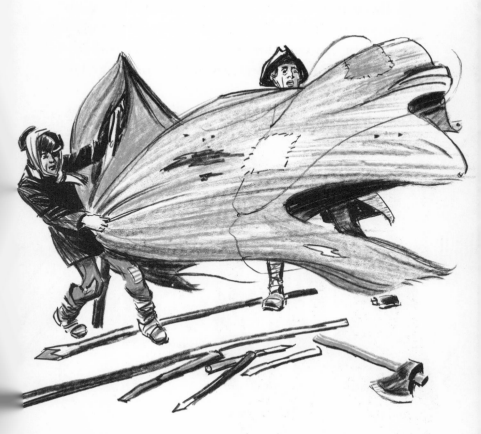

Soldiers from other states, men without shirts, shoes or blankets, must sleep on the frozen ground with only the campfires for warmth. And you can hear them talking about General Washington. For tonight the General is sleeping in a tent pitched under a gum tree nearby, even though he could have slept in a warm bed in a fine house. When a farm woman living nearby, Mrs. Deborah Hewes, came to offer the General shelter, he refused saying, "A thousand thanks, madam, but until my men have their shelters built, I'll live in my tent. I should be no warmer than they." And outside his tent, Washington raises the patriot flag

with its thirteen stars and stripes to cheer you men on.

There is little cheer tonight. The men are hungry, cold and hopeless. But you know that Washington has brought you to Valley Forge to protect the farmers and the munition factories nearby. In Philadelphia, only twenty miles away, is the British Army.

At dawn, drums beat calling you to morning roll call. You stand at attention in the snow, holding your musket with numbed fingers. Around you, are men with their ears bleeding from frostbite. Some wear tattered coats of gray, black or brown. Some officers stand at attention wearing the only covering they have: torn blankets. Many cannot report at all for they have little clothing.

Snow begins falling as you get your orders. You must build a city of huts on this hill quickly, before the snow gets too deep. General Washington has planned where each hut will stand and how it must be built. Four expert axmen and five carpenters give a lesson before each state's regiment on how to cut and notch logs, make roofs, chimneys and doors. There will be no windows — only tiny chinks between the logs to let in a bit of air.

13

The General announces a prize. He will pay the twelve dollars out of his own pocket to the first group in each regiment to finish its hut. Everyone cheers, for it has been months since Congress sent your pay.

Your regiment divides up into twelve-man squads. Farm boys like you, handy with an ax, work together chopping down forty trees to build one hut. The other fellows drag logs to the assigned spot, tying ropes across their chests to do it. Some dig up the hard ground, making mud over the fires.

The wind is fierce, but swinging an ax keeps you warm. Men work night and day, in spite of chapped faces and fingers. Some patriot farmer women living nearby welcome you by trudging through the snow with jugs of boiling coffee, pies and bread.

But the farm women cannot feed the whole
army. Soon there is so little to eat, your regiment is really fasting. All that keeps you alive
is a small ration of flour from which you make
"firecake." You mix the flour with melted snow,
spread the paste onto hot stones, and then
scrape off the thin pancake. For breakfast, din-
ner and supper you eat firecake. It keeps you
and your regiment alive.

One morning the bugle signals the battle
call. A patrol warns that thousands of British
troops are marching from Philadelphia toward
your camp. About three thousand men cannot

report for duty. They are without shoes or shirts. Those with enough clothing to march make ready, saying, "Fighting is better than starving." But the British don't come to fight, only to steal hay for their horses. They return to Philadelphia without attacking Valley Forge.

Before Christmas, food supplies run out almost completely. On Christmas Day you and the men with you chew on a few handfuls of grain. Men in other parts of the camp gnaw on bits of rotten fish. Somewhere a soldier plays his violin. Outside one hut some men try to decorate a little fir tree with odd bits of rag and metal buttons.

As powdery snows begin falling, General Washington comes riding among the tents and huts with young Lafayette at his side. Men struggle into line as they pass, standing at attention in coats of old linen tablecloths, with red woolen petticoats wrapped around their bodies, with curtains on their feet. With chattering teeth, they cheer, "Here's the General!" "Three cheers for the Commander-in-Chief!"

At night you dream about the Christmas dinners your grandmother used to make. One buddy dreams about eating a whole hog. Some men are so wracked with hunger that they sneak off to hunt rabbits and chipmunks, to steal eggs or chicken from farmers. Those caught stealing from farmers are whipped before the entire camp.

Hunger pains finally drive you men to open complaint. One day the hillsides ring out with a pitiful wail, "No meat, no meat." From tent to tent, from regiment to regiment, men hoot like angry owls or caw like crows. Officers stop the hooting with the promise that food is coming.

A messenger from Philadelphia comes into camp with a brutal report that American prisoners there are being starved to death in British prisons. Some prisoners are so maddened by hunger that they eat the clay between the bricks. Some die with pieces of bark, wood and stones in their mouths.

These reports fill you and the other men with new rage against the British. You turn your rage to good use, fiercely chopping down more trees and whittling logs for the many men still not in huts. The hard work helps you forget your empty bellies.

One day a sympathetic Englishman comes to visit with you soldiers for a while. He is Thomas Paine, the writer whose pamphlet "Common Sense" called on those who love mankind to "dare oppose the tyrant," King George III of England. To Paine, the squads of men swinging axes, hauling logs, building huts, look like a family of beavers at work in the forest.

THOMAS PAINE

Early in January, a warm sun thaws out the snows and some roads open up. Over one clear road, a band of patriot women from Philadelphia drive ten teams of oxen into camp. The animals that the good women are bringing will be slaughtered for food. With them, the women also bring two thousand shirts which they sewed and smuggled out of Philadelphia right under the noses of the British. There are cheerful songs around the campfire tonight.

Heavy January snows bury the camp in deep snow. A biting wind blows through the chinks in the hut so that anyone without a blanket would freeze. Men from three or four different huts leave their shelters to crowd around campfires all night long. Many nights they sing, and their words echo across the hill.

"Nor slaves nor cowards we will prove, Great Britain soon will see, and all the world shall know Americans are free." They sing "A

23

Toast to Washington's Health," and still another song with the words, "T'is sweet, ah, t'is sweet for our country to die."

Thousands are sick and thousands are dying from smallpox, from typhus, from frozen arms and legs. The sick fill the churches, schools, homes and barns to overflowing. Yet in the morning, when the drums call, even the sick men get up to stand in the ranks, swaying.

Every day there are new graves in the snow. Sadly you stand with the others counting the number of men buried here. One day General Washington sees the sad, despairing faces of the soldiers at their friends' graves. From then on, he orders that the graves of the thousands who die on this hill must be left unmarked so that those who live won't lose hope.

The clothing of the dead is collected, then issued to men still half-naked. Washington's scouts ride across the states urging patriots to weave cloth for the army, to give their extra coats and shoes for the scarecrow soldiers.

One bitter day in early February, you draw guard duty outside the General's headquarters. Heavy snow is falling. Through the snow, you see a horse-drawn black and tan coach draw up. Out steps a small, plump woman in a brown homespun cloak. "Would you kindly tell the General that Mrs. Washington is here?" the woman says.

You call the General quickly, for Martha Washington looks exhausted from the long journey. The General whisks his wife inside to the blazing fire, while you and the other sentries help unload her coach. It is crammed with medicines, blankets, yarns, sheets for bandages and food, taken from Mistress Washington's cupboards at Mount Vernon.

In the morning, you escort the General's lady to the huts for the sick so that she can feed the men her homemade soups and jellies. Gently she bathes the faces of the feverish men. All day for many days to come, you help carry baskets from which Mistress Washington tends the sick and hungry. Everyone soon comes to know and love her quick smile and kind brown eyes. As she passes, men call out, "God bless Mistress Washington." Those about to die call for her to comfort them and pray with them.

Soon Mistress Washington gathers officers'
wives together every morning to knit socks,
make shirts and patch breeches for the men,
and boil lengths of white cotton for bandages.
She revives hope in the men, who march past
her window singing "Yankee Doodle," the
battle song of the Revolution.

One morning a little seven-year-old Negro
girl named Mary McDonald comes trudging
through the snow to knock at Washington's
door. "I have come to join the army," the little
girl tells the sentry. Martha Washington leads
the little girl by the hand to the General, who
pats her on the head. With a smile, he gives

her permission to pass around to the men the precious potatoes, nuts and apples she carries in her apron. As Mary goes from hut to hut, the officers raise their three-cornered hats and bow low to her.

Toward the end of February, a sentry brings word to the General that Baron von Steuben is coming. Quickly the General rides down the road to welcome the heavyset Prussian soldier, a military teacher and drill master who has come to volunteer his services.

Before sunrise, the red-faced Baron is out on the parade ground drilling a hundred men in the snow. You are among those chosen. In a deep, roaring voice, the Baron calls the orders, "Fix bayonets," "Charge," "Prime and load," "Fire." If a soldier doesn't know how to

handle his musket, Steuben simply gets down off his horse, kneels in the snow and shows him. Many boys don't know how to follow simple commands like "right-face," or "left-face," for they aren't trained soldiers, but farmers and shopkeepers. Then the Baron gets red in the face, stamping his boots, waving his cane over his head, as he curses in German and French.

Finally he gets mad enough to call over his assistant, Captain Ben Walker from New York. "My dear Walker," the Baron says, "come here and swear for me in English."

Every day scores of soldiers turn out to watch Steuben drill the men chosen to be a model for the whole army. Farmers also come from miles around to watch. Only when the Baron is satisfied with his students, is General Washington invited to see the men parade and drill.

Mornings, the Baron drills regiments; afternoons, whole brigades. He teaches you to march together, turn together, fire together, and use some of the new French triangular bayonets. When you finish your training, you begin drilling others, just as the Baron showed you. Soon the spring campaign will begin; now you will be better able to fight the British, who are some of the best-trained and best-equipped soldiers in the world.

Steuben keeps you drilling, in spite of the bone-chilling March winds and sleety rains. Then suddenly a bit of grass pokes through the snow. Frogs begin croaking in the swamps.

On March 17, a clear, bright day, you hear loud, angry voices. You and your squad run over to find Irishmen from Virginia shaking their fists at a dummy hanging from a huge white oak tree. There's a piece of paper on the dummy's chest with the word PADDY painted on it.

"Dishonoring good St. Patrick, eh? We'll make them pay for it!" An angry mob begins moving toward the New England huts, for the Irishmen think the northerners strung the dummy up. Soon everyone in need of a fight takes up muskets, and a riot seems to be in the making.

Suddenly, in the midst of the shouting, drums begin beating. A tall, straight figure on horseback slowly rides into the throngs of men. A cheer breaks out, then another, and another, until soon everyone is roaring "Huzza for the General." With perfect calm, Washington sits on his horse, looking quietly at the stormy faces around him. Then he orders the whole army to take a holiday. You are among the cheering men who lay down your arms, and instead of brawling, spend the day visiting each other and playing at "long bullets" — seeing who can roll eight-pound cannon balls

farthest across the parade grounds. Other men watch a band of Captain McLane's Indian scouts. They shoot arrows at a tiny copper coin fifty yards away, hitting the mark almost every time.

One morning early in April, winter comes back. Icy blizzards howl, and the river freezes over. There's new danger the British might attack across the frozen river. Washington orders more observation posts and guards in the tallest trees. But no attack comes.

Reveille sounds one morning, and you tumble outside to find that the world has turned white with dogwood blooms. Spring is here. Men begin leaving the sick huts, and new recruits come into camp. Wagons roll in, creaking with loads of shoes and clothing.

Friendly farmers nearby come to advise that soon the fish will be running upstream. You get orders to make fishnets and to whittle long

sticks. One day the water comes alive with leaping, struggling shad. During the weeks that follow, you soldiers throng the river, catching some with your bare hands. Soldiers on horseback ride into the waters, driving the fish into nets spread across the river's mouth.

For the first time in months, every man in camp can eat his fill. Your hands and clothes reek of fish, for you help salt down hundreds of barrels to be used in the months ahead.

On May first, a messenger rides into camp bearing a sealed letter for the General. Washington breaks open the seal to learn that Benjamin Franklin has succeeded in getting the King of France to sign a treaty with the American states. France will send supplies, ships and men to help in the fighting. Young Lafayette embraces Washington, kisses him on both cheeks, and weeps with joy at the news. With France's help, there is greater hope than ever before that America will win its liberty.

There are wild cheers as the news spreads from hut to hut. Soldiers, farmers, officers, children, gather excitedly, hardly daring to believe the good news.

Washington calls for a day of prayers, parades and celebration. Every soldier must wear a sprig of flowers in his hat in honor of the French.

It is a day to remember. There are prayers of thanksgiving. Then, under a bright blue sky, you march, 11,000 men strong in two straight lines, as fifes toot and drums pound. A smile lights up the General's blue-gray eyes, for the sun bounces off your polished guns and bayonets, and you are marching in step.

Thirteen cannon shots boom out, one for each American state. Then each man in turn fires a blank charge into the air in a running fire. Loud cheers break out. "Long live the King of France! Long live the friendly powers of Europe. Huzza for the American states!"

As General Washington rides around the line, you join in a throat-splitting cheer: "Long live General Washington!"

The celebrations, cheers and toasts continue all day. There are races and games to play and extra rations to eat. As the day ends, General Washington and his lady ride down the road together to headquarters. As they pass by, cheers ring out from hut to hut. You and the others keep cheering as long as you can see your General.

In June, it is drill, drill and more drill. Patrols keep you informed of what the British Army is planning. Then one day a breathless messenger comes galloping into camp. The British are leaving the capital, Philadelphia, and are heading for New York.

Drums sound Washington's order to get ready to march. Men come running from the river, farms and hospitals. You catch up your long musket, swing your ammunition pouch over one shoulder, as the command rings out, "Brigades forward!"

Your brigade falls into step behind General Washington. As drums thunder, you march past the rows of huts, the drill ground, the trenches, and the graves of friends. Months ago, you stumbled down this road, only a boy. Today you march out a man, straight and tall, with the special pride of men who shivered, starved and still held on to the idea of freedom. You have won the right to build a new nation. There may be many struggles ahead, but nothing can stop you now.

GLOSSARY

BAYONET — a steel blade attached to the muzzle of a gun

BRIGADES — a large body of troops, usually made up of two or more regiments

CAMPAIGN — a series of military actions during a war

FIFE — a flute that is shrill in tone

FIRECAKE — a kind of pancake made of flour and water and baked on hot stones

HOMESPUN — hand-woven wool or linen that is loose in weave

MUNITIONS — bullets and other ammunition

REGIMENT — a group of soldiers made up of a number of companies and commanded by a colonel

SENTRIES — soldiers standing guard at a particular point

SHAD — a type of fish common in North America. It is something like a herring.

SICK HUTS — log cabins that served as hospitals

TYPHUS — a disease which causes high fever. It is carried by body lice.

TYRANT — a dictator or a ruler who has complete power over his people

Other Things to Do While Reading *With Washington at Valley Forge*

1. Report on Thomas Paine and his part in the American Revolution.
2. Find out more about Lafayette and how he helped the Americans.
3. Make a report on Baron von Steuben and how he helped the Americans.
4. List at least fifteen or twenty words or phrases in this book that make you feel cold.
5. List at least ten or fifteen words or phrases from this book that make you feel hungry.
6. Locate at least three Revolutionary War songs, such as "Yankee Doodle," and learn the words and melodies.
7. Draw pictures of the British uniforms during the Revolutionary War.
8. List the weapons that the rebels had. Explain how each weapon works.
9. Write a paragraph describing how the starving, freezing men at Valley Forge found ways of keeping up their spirits.
10. Report on typhus and smallpox, diseases which attacked the men camping at Valley Forge.
11. Learn some simple military commands from a member of the R.O.T.C. or from a soldier.
12. Which colonies are mentioned in this book?

Another Book About Valley Forge:
Meadowcroft, Enid, *Silver for General Washington*. New York, Thomas Y. Crowell Company, 1957.

Other Books On
Building America

Drake Digs for Oil

The First Transcontinental Railroad

With Lewis and Clark

The Louisiana Purchase

Down the Mississippi With LaSalle

The First Independence Day

The Klondike Gold Rush

At Plymouth With the Pilgrims

With Paul Revere

The Battle of Gettysburg

Exploring With Magellan

DATE DUE

MR 17 '69 61
AP 29 '69 61
OCT 14 '69 31
JA 22 '70 33
APR 16 '70 52
APR 23 '70 58
OCT 15 '70 42
NOV 6 '78 42
APR 21 '71 46
APR 27 '72 44
MAY 11 '72 44

52.250